OUT OF THIS WORLD Jokes & Riddles

MICHAEL J. PELLOWSKI

STERLING CHILDREN'S BOOKS
New York

To Skyeler E.J. & Loukas Morgan Pellowski

STERLING CHILDREN'S BOOKS
New York

An Imprint of Sterling Publishing Co., Inc.
1166 Avenue of the Americas
New York, NY 10036

STERLING CHILDREN'S BOOKS and the distinctive Sterling Children's Books logo
are registered trademarks of Sterling Publishing Co., Inc.

ISBN 978-1-4549-2257-5

Distributed in Canada by Sterling Publishing Co., Inc.
c/o Canadian Manda Group, 664 Annette Street
Toronto, Ontario, Canada M6S 2C8
Distributed in the United Kingdom by GMC Distribution Services
Castle Place, 166 High Street, Lewes, East Sussex, England BN7 1XU

For information about custom editions, special sales, and premium and
corporate purchases, please contact Sterling Special Sales at 800-805-5489 or
specialsales@sterlingpublishing.com.

Manufactured in Canada

Lot #:
2 4 6 8 10 9 7 5 3 1
03/17

www.sterlingpublishing.com

Design by Ryan Thomann

Contents

HA HA HA

HA HA HA

1

THAT'S THEORY FUNNY

Shelly: If you invite one cousin to your birthday party, you have to invite all your cousins.
LENNY: Is that some kind of birthday rule?
SHELLY: No. It's my birthday theory of relativity.

How did the Green Giant become a physicist?
He earned his Pea H. D.

HA HA HA

HA HA HA

How long does it take a physicist to shoot a basketball free throw?

Ten minutes and ten seconds. Ten minutes to work out the equation for the correct trajectory of the ball, and ten seconds to make the shot.

What did the physicist have with his cheeseburger?

Sci-fries.

INSTRUCTOR: Use the word *cosmos* in a sentence.

STUDENT: Slippery road conditions *cosmos* car accidents.

Knock-knock!

Who's there?

My crow.

My crow who?

My crow biology.

Which scientist is always giggling?

The par-tickle physicist.

Why did the physicist walk to the top of the Empire State Building instead of taking the elevator?

She was a stair trek fan.

Show me a physicist who becomes a trapeze artist . . . and I'll show you an acrobat with a high IQ.

What do you call a scientist who studies soda pop?

A fizzicist.

Knock-knock!

Who's there?

Albert.

Albert who?

Albert you think my last name is Einstein.

BRAIN BUSTER

Does a smart cyclops have a high eye-Q?

What do you get when you cross a physicist with a witch?

A person who conducts scientific hexperiments.

○   ○

SIGN ON AN EXPERIMENTAL PHYSICIST'S DOOR

Gone fission!

Knock-knock!

Who's there?

Theory.

Theory who?

Theory goes again, bragging about how smart he is.

DAFFYNITION

Archaeology student:

a person whose future is in the past

What do you shout to a physicist playing in a heavy metal band?

Rock it, scientist!

BRAIN BUSTER

Does a person need a master's degree
to work at a dog obedience school?

Knock-knock!

Who's there?

Dewey Noah.

Dewey Noah who?

Dewey Noah solution to that equation?

ROG: I've never been late to any of my college classes.

JESS: What a conscientious student you are!

ROG: I'm the professor. I can't afford to be tardy!

SCIENTIST: I think the object in space we discovered is an asteroid. What do you think?

PHYSICIST: No comet.

What does caveman Albert Einstein carry?

A science club.

What do you call it when a physicist's uncle initiates a round of golf?

Relative-at-tee.

BENNY: I'm studying the primitive locomotion of fleas.

LENNY: Well, don't jump to any conclusions.

SHELLY: I have a theory that all ornate doorknockers are obsolete.

KELLY: What are you trying to do, win a no-bell prize?

What do you get when you cross a primitive android with a clock?

Robot-ticks.

STAFF MEETING

Professor B. A. Cannon—she's an advocate of the Big Bang Theory.

Dr. Ben A. Bridegroom—he proposes a lot of radical theories.

Dr. Teeny Little—she's in charge of a government weesearch program.

Dr. I. M. Farrout—he's the head of deep-space exploration.

Who lives in a bottle, works magic, and has a high IQ?

A genie-us.

LENNY: I'm studying the effect of severe poison ivy on cognitive thinking.

BENNY: Well, don't make any rash judgments.

What did one time traveler say to the other time traveler when they met in the future?

"Good-bye. I'll see you yesterday."

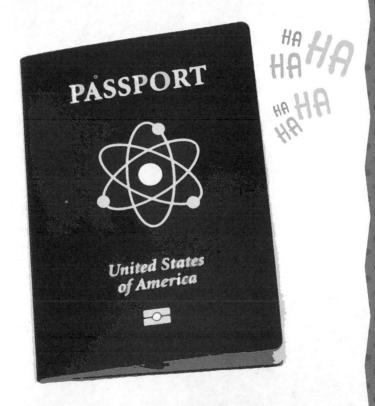

Knock-knock!
    Who's there?
Tree.
    Tree who?
Tree! Two! One!
Blast off!

Knock-knock!
    Who's there?
Hy.
    Hy who?
Hy IQ.

Knock-knock!
    Who's there?
Sy.
    Sy who?
Sy-ience class.

Knock-knock!
    Who's there?
Faye.
    Faye who?
Faye-zers at stun
level, Captain.

BENNY: I want to learn
everything there is to know
about stomach ailments.
LENNY: What has that got
to do with science?
BENNY: It's quantummy
physics.

NELLIE: I'm so smart, I can read your mind.
KELLY: I'm smart, too, but I can't read your mind. The print is too small.

What do you call a physicist's female sibling?
   A physister.

PROFESSOR HIP-HOP'S RAP THEORY:
"E=MC Hammer"

How do you mend a broken periodic table?
   Use perio-duct tape.

What do you call a brain operation on a Roman Emperor?
   Nero-surgery.

JACK: Do you even know what an IQ is?

ZACK: No. And I can't spell it either.

What group did the snobby computer experts belong to?

They were in a "click."

HORTON: I'm the smartest person in the world. I never forget anything.

NORTON: Don't be so conceited. Your ego is out of control. You need to rethink that boastful claim.

HORTON: Oh, you've got me all upset. Now what was I saying?

Did you hear about the Green Giant scientist named Paul Bunyan who became a gourmet chef and cooked up a pea-tree dish?

SCIENTIST: Are you cooking something?

PHYSICIST: Yes. I'm trying different natural additives to increase the flavor of the meal I'm preparing.

SCIENTIST: Oh! So this is a case of spice exploration.

FRANZ: I'll have you know physics is a science that deals with matter and its interactions.

HANS: Well, it doesn't matter to me because I don't have the energy to discuss it with you.

What is an archaeologist?
A scientist who lives in the past.

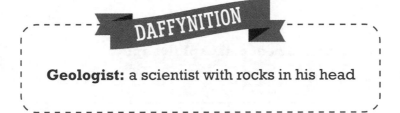

Is oceanography a science for deep-sea thinkers?

What is a physicist's favorite horror story?
Dr. Jekyll and Mr. Hydrogen.

PONDER PUNCH

Sweet potato philosophy:
I think, therefore I yam.

Knock-knock!
  Who's there?
Ida Teacher.
  Ida Teacher who?
Ida Teacher who once told me I was the best
student she ever had.

LENNY: If you were a space pirate, would you carry a heavy sword?
SHELLY: No. I'd use a light saber.

Why did the anatomy student decide to become a podiatrist?

She wanted to start her medical career at the bottom and work her way up.

2

What does a chemist wear in December?
A winter lab coat.

Which radio station do astrophysicists listen to?
The International Space Station.

What do you get when a college instructor falls down a flight of stairs?
A professore.

BRAIN BUSTER

Do audio researchers make sound judgments?

Knock-knock!
Who's there?
Al.
Al who?
Al-gebraic numbers.

KNOCK-KNOCK!

BRIGHT BOY: Are you a well-read person?

DIMWIT: No. I feel ill if I get sunburned.

What advanced math did Professor Magician teach?

Trickonometry.

Knock-knock!

Who's there?

Laser beam.

Laser beam who?

Laser beam me up, Scotty!

What physicist was an expert on the cookie theory?

Sir Isaac Fig Newton.

Show me a group of untidy dinosaurs . . . and I'll show you giant reptiles that lived during the Messyzoic Era.

HA HA HA HA HA HA HA HA HA

What did Venus say to Saturn?

"**Hey there! Give me a ring sometime.**"

What did Daffy and Donald earn in grad school?

Their ducktorate degrees.

LESTER: I never make mistakes because I have a photographic memory.
CHESTER: Baloney! That doesn't mean you're always picture-perfect.

PROFESSORS' ROLL CALL

Dr. U. R. Wong

Dr. I. M. Wright

Dr. I. Noah Itall

Dr. Jeanie Uss

Dr. Les R. Beam

Dr. P. H. Dee

Knock-knock!

Who's there?

I. M. Graduate.

I. M. Graduate who?

I. M. Graduate all your dinner.

DAFFYNITION

Geology Class: learning the hard way

What do you get when you cross the world's fastest human with the world's smartest student?

A pupil who is a really quick study.

LENNY: I heard Professor Freeze had a panic attack in the lab.

SHELLY: Yes. He suffered a complete meltdown.

Why did the genius take a jump rope to school?

She wanted to skip a few grades.

BULLY: Listen, wise guy, you have a smart mouth.

BRAINY: I have a smart everything. My IQ is 180.

What do you call a nerdy physicist?

An expert on dork matter.

HERMAN: Do you want to know something?

SHERMAN: No. I already know everything.

Why did Astronaut Santa fail to deliver any Christmas gifts?

He flew into a black ho-ho-hole.

Why couldn't the senior doctor of philosophy learn to do a handstand?

Because you can't teach an old doc new tricks.

Knock-knock!

Who's there?

Artie.

Artie who?

Artie-ficial intelligence.

KNOCK-KNOCK!

CHESTER: Do physicists like physical contests?

LESTER: No. They prefer mind games.

KOOKY QUESTION

Does the planet Saturn have a unique ringtone?

What is furry and very smart?

A brainy-yak.

SHELLY: I keep thinking about what will happen if the world runs out of H2O.

LENNY: Oh stop it, or you'll end up with water on the brain.

HERMAN: I challenge you to a battle of wits.

SHERMAN: Sorry. I refuse to compete against an unarmed foe.

What do you get when you cross a chemistry experiment with a potato?

A test tuber.

Show me a brainy hog farmer ... and I'll show you an excellent speaker of Pig Latin.

Why does Mr. Spock eat almonds first, cashews next, and pistachios last?

It's nut logical.

LENNY: What job would you have if you were in the army?

SHELLY: I'd drive a think tank.

Knock-knock!

Who's there?

Newt.

Newt who?

Newt-ron.

HERMAN: Why did you throw away your new phone?

SHERMAN: It wasn't smart enough to be seen in my company.

What do you get when you cross a physicist with a violin virtuoso?

An expert on string theory.

MACK: I'm an aeronautical engineer.

ZACK: Humph! You're just another airhead to me.

PENNY: I just saw a meteorite.

JENNY: Nope. What you saw was a comet.

PENNY: Oh well. I guess I was meteor-wrong.

What do you get when you cross an oak tree with a college instructor?

A nutty professor.

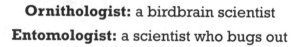

DAFFYNITIONS

Ornithologist: a birdbrain scientist

Entomologist: a scientist who bugs out

LESTER: How did you ever get a job as an electrical engineer?

CHESTER: I have a lot of positive connections.

THE GOOFY GALAXY

What did the doctor give the astronaut before liftoff?

A booster shot.

Why did the satellite break out of its orbit?

It wanted its own space.

Which planet smells the best?

The sun. It's the scenter of our universe.

How did Mars become the red planet?

It stayed out in the sun too long.

What would you call an ocean on the moon?

Luna sea.

What did the meteor say to the earth's atmosphere?

"You burn me up!"

3

FUNNY PHYSICS

What do you get when you cross a crop-grower with a chemist?
A farmacist.

What do Mickey and Minnie look through to examine tiny specimens?
They look through their mice-roscopes.

SHELLY: Did you know argon is a gas?
NELLIE: No. I thought it was a character from *The Lord of the Rings*.

Which robot dances in Swan Lake?
R2 D-TUTU.

Why do you need an astronaut maid on a space station?
Because a space station has a lot of stardust.

Why did Professor Dorky go to Athens?
He wanted to study geek mythology.

Why couldn't Professor Dorky solve the mystery of Pharaoh's tomb?
He was clueless.

Then there was the expert string theorist who couldn't tie his shoelaces.

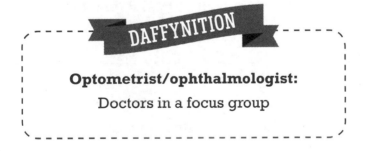

DAFFYNITION

Optometrist/ophthalmologist:
Doctors in a focus group

What do you call it when Mickey and Donald get in trouble at Cartoon College?
Suspended animation.

LENNY: You'll never guess who works in the Star Wars restaurant.
PENNY: Who?
LENNY: Darth Waiter.

HA HA HA HA HA HA HA HA HA

Knock-knock!
  Who's there?
Ed Hugh.
  Ed Hugh who?
Ed Hugh Cation.

DAFFYNITIONS

Control group: members of the family who monopolize the TV remote
Podiatrist: a medical heeler

Why was the zombie astronaut famous?
  He was the first creature to take an undead walk in space.

What is the best way to illuminate a black hole?
  Turn on a bunch of satellites.

ROG: What does your father do for a living?

JESS: He's a salesman.

ROG: Does he sell a lot of different things?

JESS: No. He only sells computers. Nothing else.

ROG: Oh! So he's sort of a one-sell organism.

Why are helium, neon, argon, krypton, radon, and xenon considered to be members of a royal family?

They are all noble gases.

SHELLY: Lenny is so out of shape, the university lab paid him *not* to donate his body to science.

What kind of space fish do you find in our solar system?

Neptuna.

When does the entire solar system celebrate?

When a star is born.

What did one hippie atom say to the other hippie atom?

Hey, dude! Let's split!

CHESTER: Would you like to hear an asteroid story?

LESTER: Not really. I'd much rather hear a comet tale.

What do you call very dull extraterrestrials?
   Star bores.

BRAIN BUSTER

Is it true you can determine how old the planet Saturn is by counting its rings and multiplying the sum by a million?

Show me a chemistry student who snitches on his fellow pupils . . . and I'll show you a lab rat.

Who is in charge of the science troop?
   The biology major.

LENNY: Is that a nuclear-powered baby cradle?

DENNY: No. It's just old-fashioned rock-it science.

What is an astrophysicist's favorite rhyme to sing?
   "Moon Rover, Moon Rover, can a space probe come over?"

Where does an astronaut keep a peanut-butter-and-jelly sandwich?

In her launch bag.

————— BRAIN BUSTER —————

Is the constellation Pisces really a starfish?

AMY: A solar flare is a giant magnetic arch.

JAMIE: Are you trying to attract my attention by telling me that?

————— BRAIN BUSTER —————

Do professors who study magnetic fields have a lot of pull at the university?

HOWIE: That new grad student is not very bright.

BARRY: What makes you say that?

HOWIE: I told her she could take a make-up exam, and she brought a cosmetic case to class.

What has fewer calories than a full moon?

Moonlite.

SHELLY: When I was two years old, I learned to count up to 180.

LENNY: Wow! But why 180?

SHELLY: Simple. That was my IQ at the time.

BRAIN BUSTER

Do overweight robots like heavy-metal music?

What do an algebra teacher and a geometry instructor do when they go fishing together?

They throw in parallel lines.

Knock-knock!

Who's there?

Cosmo.

Cosmo who?

Cosmo-chemistry deals with the chemical composition of the universe.

KNOCK-KNOCK!

LENNY: That girl is so conceited. She thinks all the planets revolve around her.

SHELLY: Does she not have a rudimentary grasp of how our solar system operates?

BRAIN BUSTER

Is counterintelligence a polite way of
saying a person is not very smart?

How do you locate a lost star?
Follow its star tracks.

HA HA HA HA HA

*Then there was the uncool mathematician who
became a cheerleader so she could lead all the
square roots.*

Why did the atom go on a diet?
Its molecular weight was too heavy.

BARRY: I have a PhD in thermal dynamics.
HOWIE: So I guess you think you're hot stuff.

Why did Orville and Wilbur do so well in geometry?
They were both experts on Wright triangles.

Knock-knock!
Who's there?
Oscar.
Oscar who?
Oscar if she knows anything about string theory.

JENNY: Which planet is always hopping mad?
PENNY: Jumping Jupiter! I have no idea.

LENNY: Why are you having fast food for lunch? I thought you were concerned about proper nutrition.
SHELLY: Because I only have time for a quick bite before I run to a lecture posthaste.

HOWIE: Do astronauts drink coffee in space?
BARRY: No. They prefer E-tea.

BRIGHT BERNIE: Quasars are stars that send out powerful radio waves.
DENSE DANNY: What type of music do they play?

BRAIN BUSTER

Do fizz ed teachers give pop quizzes?

SHELLY: Who was the wimpiest president of the United States?
NELLIE: Calvin Un-Coolidge.

—————— BRAIN BUSTER ——————
Did you hear about the math detective
who couldn't solve a crime because
none of his clues ever added up?

Why did the student bring his camera to biology?
**Because his class was studying
photosynthesis.**

ROG: I have a theory that eating a banana a day increases a person's IQ.
JESS: Why didn't you propose that concept to the college dietitian when we met her this morning?
ROG: I guess it just slipped my mind.

Knock-knock!

Who's there?

Stu.

Stu who?

Stu-dents belong in school.

BRAIN BUSTER

Does a Saturn shirt have a ring around its collar?

BARRY: Is Venus a planet or a star?

HOWIE: She's a star. In fact, she's a tennis star. So is her sister Serena.

Why did the silly grad student take his exam to dinner and a movie?

His professor told him to date his test.

Which brainy dinosaur knows a lot of words?

The thesaurus.

JENNY: Did you know most meteors are no bigger than a pea?

PENNY: Humph! And who told you that? The Green Giant Astronomer?

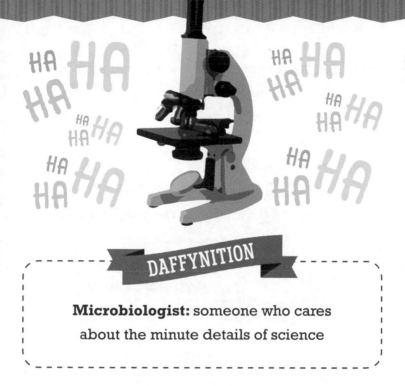

Microbiologist: someone who cares about the minute details of science

What do you get when you cross a lunar astronaut with a geologist?

A space man with moon rocks in his head.

JENNY: Penny, please boil some water for me.
PENNY: Okay. What's the recipe?

BRIGHT BERNIE: The Oort Cloud is a mysterious giant halo that surrounds our solar system.
DENSE DANNY: We oort to know more about it than we do.

SHELLY: Now, to continue my lecture, a super nova is an exploding star.

LENNY: Ugh! If you don't stop talking, my head will explode!

CHESTER: I'm an ornithologist. I study birds.

LESTER: I guess you think that's a feather in your cap.

How do you clean an asteroid?

Put it through a meteor shower.

What do you get when you cross Captain Kirk with Sabrina the teenage witch?

Star Trek: The Hex Generation.

HA HA HA HA HA HA HA HA HA HA HA HA

LEARNED LENNY: Why are you holding your socks and shoes and walking barefoot through the snow?

SILLY SHELLY: Because if I get my socks and shoes wet, I might catch a cold.

LENNY: Which would you rather be: a red star, or a blue star?

PENNY: I don't know. What's the difference?

LENNY: Well, red stars are the coolest, and blue stars are the hottest.

PENNY: In that case, I guess I'm both.

HA HA HA HA HA HA

4

DON'T KNOCK KNOWLEDGE

Scientist: What part of blasting into space frightens you most?

ASTRONAUT: I'm not sure. I guess it's the atmos-fear.

Knock-knock!

Who's there?

I, senior.

I, senior who?

I senior grades, and they're good enough to get you into an Ivy League school.

Knock-knock!
Who's there?
Alex.
Alex who?
Alex you a question, and you have ten seconds to answer it.

HA HA HA HA HA

Knock-knock!
Who's there?
Frosh.
Frosh who?
Frosh flowers wilt if you don't put them in water.

Knock-knock!
Who's there?
Allied.
Allied who?
Allied when I said I have a PhD. I only have a master's degree.

Knock-knock!

Who's there?

Phyllis.

Phyllis who?

Phyllis in on the results of your latest experiment.

HA HA HA HA HA HA

What college did the king's son graduate from?

Princeton.

Knock-knock!

Who's there?

Thesis.

Thesis who?

Thesis a stickup!

Knock-knock!

Who's there?

Telly.

Telly who?

Telly scope.

Knock-knock!

Who's there?

Amos.

Amos who?

Amos study hard if I want to earn a PhD.

What college did the chai latte graduate from?
MI-Tea.

Knock-knock!
Who's there?
Thermos.
Thermos who?
Thermos be a solution to this complex equation.

Knock-knock!
Who's there?
R. Soul.
R. Soul who?
R. Soul-er system is a collection of planets revolving around the sun.

Knock-knock!
Who's there?
Dozen.
Dozen who?
Dozen anyone know the answer to my question?

What college did Yogi and Boo-Boo graduate from?
Brown Bear University.

HA HA HA

Knock-knock!
Who's there?
A mole.
A mole who?
A mole-cule.

Knock-knock!
Who's there?
Phil.
Phil who?
Phil-osophy is for
deep thinkers.

What college
did the mermaid
graduate from?
US-Sea.

Knock-knock!
Who's there?
Anita.
Anita who?
Anita quiet place to
study for exams.

HA HA HA
HA HA HA
HA HA HA
HA HA
HA HA

Knock-knock!
  Who's there?
Eclipse.
  Eclipse who?
Eclipse my hair when it gets too long.

Knock-knock!
  Who's there?
Shirley.
  Shirley who?
Shirley you must know the answer to this simple question.

Knock-knock!
  Who's there?
Jess.
  Jess who?
Jess sit quietly while I finish my lecture.

HA HA HA HA HA HA HA HA HA HA HA HA

What is the one type of college you should avoid?
Poison Ivy League schools.

HA HA HA

5

BIG BANG BONKERS

Morgan: What do you get when you cross a leading actor with Dungeons & Dragons?

GORDON: What?

MORGAN: A starring role-playing game.

What do you get when you cross a boy wizard with a popular craft store?

Harry Pottery Barn.

What do you get when the starship *Enterprise*'s medical officer falls down a flight of stairs?

Broken Bones McCoy.

SHELLY: I made an android goat.
LENNY: Oh really? Is it a robutter?

What card game do grad students like to play?

Five-Card Study.

HA HA HA HA HA

DAFFYNITION

Unmarried male physicist:
a bachelor of science

What's the biggest problem the Abominable Snow Physicist has?

Brain freezes.

Then there was the hi-tech crow physicist who had cawer ID on his smartphone.

What does a Neanderthal physicist carry?

A science club.

Why didn't the boy pharmacist marry the girl pharmacist?

Their chemistry just wasn't right.

LOONY LOGIC

If a tree falls in the forest and no one's there to hear it, who cares?

NELLIE: My favorite auntie is Auntie Melanie. Who is your favorite auntie?

SHELLY: Auntie-septic. I have a germ phobia.

What do you call a scientist who studies pecans, cashews, and almonds?

An internut explorer.

What do you get when you cross a saline solution with a goofy cartoon duck?

Salt Water Daffy.

BRAIN BUSTER

When a fizzicist wants to get engaged, does he pop the question?

Knock-knock!

Who's there?

Anna.

Anna who?

Anna-lyze my problems.

What did the dopey dinosaur end up as?

A fossil fool.

HOWIE: More than 70 percent of the earth's surface is covered in water.

BARRY: I'll drink to that!

THE OLD COLLEGE TRY

What college did Aladdin's genie graduate from?
   The University of Wish-consin.

What college do tailors go to?
   The University of Pantsylvania.

Where did Mickey, Pluto, and Donald go to college?
   The University of Minnie-sota.

Where did Professor Peach go to college?
   The University of Pitsburgh.

What college did Noah graduate from?
   The University of Arkansas.

Where did Professor Orange graduate from?
   The Navel Academy.

Which school is the best place to study raising cheap feed for cows and horses?
   UCL-Hay.

Which southern school has a
flawless Olympic score?
Perfect Ten-essee.

What college did Professor
Gazelle graduate from?
Gnu Mexico State.

Where do watchmen earn their college credits?
At Cal-Tick.

Which college football team does Aladdin's genie
root for?
The Ali-Bama Crimson Tide.

LENNY: Did Popeye the Sailor earn
top grades in college?
PENNY: No. He was a sea student.

AMY: Did you graduate from sky-diving school?
JAMIE: No. I dropped out.

HOWIE: I took a cooking class on how to prepare steaks.
BARRY: How did you do?
HOWIE: I didn't make the cut.

ROG: I took a class on forestry management.
JESS: How did you do?
ROG: I felled the class.

Which canine has a college degree?
The Yale Bulldog.

What is formal attire for an astronaut?
Spacesuit and tie.

PENNY: I took an Internet course on grammar and spelling.

DENNY: How did you do?

PENNY: I was WordPerfect.

LENNY: How are you doing in astronautics class?

JENNY: My grades are out of this world.

SHELLY: How are your grades in geology class?

NELLIE: They're rock solid.

DR. JONES: Why are you jogging at midnight, Professor Smith?

PROF. SMITH: All of my lectures were too long today, so tonight I'm running late.

KOOKIE COMPUTER DATED

Professor Ancient is so old, he remembers when a notebook was something you wrote in with a pencil.

Professor Ancient is so old, he remembers when spell-check was the dictionary.

Professor Ancient is so old, he remembers when a mouse was something a cat chased.

BERNIE: How did you do in your marine biology course last semester?

ERNIE: My grades took a nosedive, and now I'm in deep trouble.

BERNIE: Are you studying blood pressure in medical school?

ERNIE: Yes. And my grade keeps going up, up, up!

What do you get when you cross severe flu symptoms with cream cheese?

Germs that spread easily.

Knock-knock!

Who's there?

Louis Pasteur.

Louis Pasteur who?

Louis Pasteur, because she was driving too slowly.

Pediatrician: a doctor who likes to kid around with medicine

Knock-knock!

Who's there?

Sulfur.

Sulfur who?

Sulfur the last two years I've been studying for my doctorate.

KNOCK-KNOCK!

Then there was the nervous scientist who refused to study earthquakes because they sent shivers down his spine.

LENNY: Do you keep your old exams in that trunk?
SHELLY: Yes. It's my test case.

THE PHILOSOPHY OF DESCARTES THE SKUNK:

"I stink, therefore I am."

DR. SMITH: I'm a psychiatrist.
STUDENT: Well, what do you think of that?
DR. SMITH: You tell me.

Why is a microbiologist like a prison guard?
They both spend a lot of time examining cells.

Knock-knock!

Who's there?

Aorta.

Aorta who?

Aorta go home and study for tomorrow's exam.

HA HA HA HA HA HA

LENNY: What were you doing in the lab?

BENNY: I was experimenting with a new kind of toy.

LENNY: Oh yeah? What kind?

BENNY: A chemical-reaction figure.

What do you get when you cross a ton of NaCl with a hog farm?

Lots of salt pork.

What do you get when you cross a podiatrist with an oral surgeon?

A doctor who specializes in foot-in-mouth ailments.

What do you get when you cross an artist with a mathematician?

Someone who paints by numbers.

Knock-knock!

Who's there?

Armageddon.

Armageddon who?

Armageddon tired of repeating this experiment and expecting a different result.

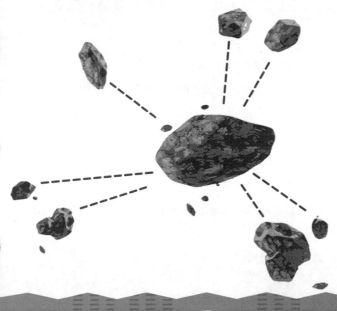

6

Who has red hair and button eyes and fights diseases?
Little Orphan Antibody.

Knock-knock!
Who's there?
Earl E. Tibet.
Earl E. Tibet who?
Earl E. Tibet and early to rise makes your brain healthy and wise.

SHELLY: How did you ace your geology exam?

NELLIE: I studied hard for it.

PHYSICIST: Do you use ant traps in your work?

ENTOMOLOGIST: No. They're too tiny to bait.

AMY: I crossbred an octopus with a boxing ape.

JAMIE: What did you get?

AMY: A well-armed gorilla fighter.

Knock-knock!

Who's there?

Hugh Tortoise.

Hugh Tortoise who?

Hugh Tortoise everything we know about physics.

What kind of doctor has an office in Egypt?

A Cairo-practor.

Knock-knock!

Who's there?

Yukon.

Yukon who?

Yukon earn a good grade in physics class if you study.

Why didn't the algebra teacher and the calculus instructor get along?

They just couldn't figure each other out.

————————— **BRAIN BUSTER** —————————

Are academically unchallenged
students members of the school bored?

Which college graduate works in an ice cream shop?

The sundae school teacher.

What does a Martian lumberjack use to fell space trees?

An axe-ray.

Knock-knock!

Who's there?

Water.

Water who?

Water you studying in college?

BERNIE: What do you get when you cross an electrical engineer and a hydraulics expert?
ERNIE: Shock waves.

Why is a university like a kingdom?

They both have lots of subjects.

———————— **BRAIN BUSTER** ————————

Do dental students take oral exams?

What does an art teacher do before classes start?

Draws up lesson plans.

What do three classroom feet add up to?

A school yard.

What do you get when you cross an architect with a mathematician?

Home additions.

Why did the dentist go back to college?

He wanted to brush up on his studies.

Then there was the optician who moonlighted as a stand-up comedian and used a lot of sight gags in his act.

What's the best way to study for a theology exam?
  Form a soul support group.

SHELLY: I think I'm allergic to bees.
LENNY: What makes you say that?
SHELLY: Every time I see one, I break out in hives.

What did one Internet browser say to the other?
  "First come, first surfed."

What do you get when you cross a contented cat with a doctor's medical note?
  A purrscription.

How many rocks should a thirsty geologist collect?
  Two quartz.

LENNY: Did you meet that famous snobby architect?

SHELLY: Yes. And in my opinion, he's too big for his own bridges.

ROG: How old is our universe?

JESS: It's so old, the Milky Way is turning into sour cream.

WHAT'S ON YOUR MIND?

- -

What did the psychiatrist say to the neurotic suitcase salesman?

> **"Get a grip on yourself."**

What did the psychiatrist say to neurotic Bugs Bunny?

> **"Think hoppy thoughts."**

What did the psychiatrist say to the neurotic chef?

> **"Just simmer down."**

What did the psychiatrist say to the duck with ruffled feathers?

> **"Just calm down."**

HA HA HA HA   HA HA HA HA

What do you get when you cross Captain Kirk with the Flash?

A star fleet-footed hero.

Why does Saturn have a ring?

Because it's engaged to Mars.

Why did the pollster go to a psychiatrist?

Because he lost his census.

Knock-knock!

Who's there?

Savior.

Savior who?

Savior energy or we'll suffer a blackout.

MEDICAL PROFESSOR: Do you have a scalpel?
ANATOMY STUDENT: No, but I have a shoulder blade.

What did one centrifuge say to the other centrifuge?

"One good turn deserves another."

BARRY: Did you hear about the architect who wants to erect a bridge across the Mediterranean?

HARRY: Yes. I saw the story on SEA-SPAN.

Knock-knock!

Who's there?

Isle.

Isle who?

Isle see you in chemistry class.

KNOCK-KNOCK!

COLETTE: You mean he's not a real microbiologist?

BERNADETTE: That's right! He's a micro-phony!

What do you get when you cross an agricultural student with a sour pickle?

The Farmer in the Dill.

What do you get when you cross a tall, happy farmer with a field of wheat?

The Jolly Grain Giant.

SHELDON: What happened to the centrifuge that was in the lab?

BELDON: I think someone took it out for a spin.

SHELLY: Why don't ants go out at night?

PENNY: Because uncles like to stay home and watch sports on TV.

What do you get when you cross an art professor with a hydraulics expert?

An artist who likes to draw water.

Then there was the music major who kept bringing his college professor notes from home.

Why is an optometrist like a college professor?

They both examine a lot of pupils.

ROG: How did you pass your culinary arts exam?

JESS: I cooked up some really good answers.

7

DO YOU THINK THAT'S AMUSING?

Who was the first dog on the moon?
The lunar rover.

HOWIE: I'm going to invest in a comic book store.
BARRY: What condition is it in?
HOWIE: Mint.

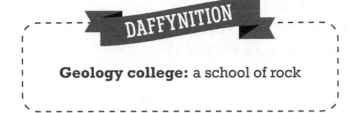
MARTY: I'm sure glad I'm not a Russian physicist.
ARTIE: Why is that?
MARTY: I don't speak Russian.

PROFESSOR MATTHEWS: Shelly has such a big ego, she'd never let them clone her. She says you can't duplicate perfection.

Knock-knock!
    Who's there?
Beehive.
    Beehive who?
Beehive yourself or leave the classroom.

Then there was the explorer who took a mountain-climbing class but couldn't make the grade.

JUDY: Do you think I'll like art appreciation class?
TRUDIE: You'll have to draw your own conclusion.

MACK: Why did you stop taking pre-med classes?
ZACK: They started to make me sick.

Show me a theology student who also took courses in military tactics . . . and I'll show you a member of the Salvation Army.

SHELLY: A genius like me would never blend in at a fitness club.
NELLIE: Why not?
SHELLY: The place is full of dumbbells.

DENNY: Would you like to take a spin class to get in shape?
LENNY: The only spin class that interests me is one that revolves around a centrifuge.

Knock-knock!
>**Who's there?**

Art and Jim.
>**Art and Jim who?**

Art and Jim classes are lots of fun.

PROFESSOR SKYLER: Morgan has a family history when it comes to geology. He comes from a long line of famous geologists. In fact, he can trace the roots of his family tree back to a petrified forest.

KNOCK-KNOCK!

--- **BRAIN BUSTER** ---

Is earth science a dirty textbook?

KNOW KIDDING

Years ago, parents used to boast "My kid is smarter than your kid!" Today, kids boast "My phone is smarter than your phone!"

AMY: Last night my genius boyfriend took me out for some late-night stargazing.

JAMIE: Gee! That sounds romantic and exciting.

AMY: Not really. He wouldn't share his telescope.

Then there was the atom researcher who needed to see a psychiatrist because of his split personality.

BENNY: Do you have trouble counting how many chin-ups you can do?

LENNY: No. It's real easy.

BENNY: How can it be so easy?

LENNY: Well, I can only do one.

NICK: I'm an EMT for the college marching band.

RICK: Exactly what service do you provide?

NICK: Band Aid.

INVENTION CONVENTION

Dynamite: Alfred Nobel's blasted invention

Lightning rod: an invention Ben Franklin brainstormed

Machine gun: a military invention that caused Richard Gatling to get fired! Fired! Fired!

Evolution: Darwin's theory that tried to make monkeys out of a lot of scientists

Electric lightbulb: Thomas Edison's bright idea

Knock-knock!

Who's there?

Comma.

Comma who?

Comma over here and sit down.

Then there was the aspiring judge who flunked his bar exam essay because his sentences were too short.

KNOCK-KNOCK!

8

GALAXY GRINS

Who do you get when you cross a bum with a *Star Wars* bounty hunter?

Hobo Fett.

What is the moon's favorite letter of the alphabet?

Luna C.

Why is the planet Saturn like a big circus?
They both have multiple rings.

STARRY BOOK TITLE
The Vastness of Space
by Galex Cee

BARRY: If you wanted to buy a neutrino, how much would it cost?
HOWIE: Nothing. A neutrino is an elementary particle free of charge.

SIGN IN A ROCKET SCIENCE CLASSROOM
This is not a crash course!

What do you call four theoretical physicists?
A string quartet.

What did James Kirk sit on while in the alien forest?

The captain's log.

JENNY: Have you ever heard of Dr. Cobbler?
LENNY: No. What did he do?
JENNY: He heeled a lot of sick people.

What was Pavlov's favorite fast food?
Kentucky Freud Chicken.

SHELLY: Is there such a thing as a high school neutrino?
LENNY: No. A neutrino is an elementary particle.

Then there was the near-sighted sailor who went to an optometrist because he was really see-sick.

What school do tired college students attend?
The University of Rest Virginia.

SHELLY: A genius like myself can make educated predictions that are almost always accurate.

LENNY: Really?

SHELLY: Of course!

LENNY: Do you think it's going to rain this weekend?

SHELLY: How the heck should I know?

Knock-knock!

Who's there?

Hugh.

Hugh who?

Hugh-tube.

What kind of food supplement should you take if you're just too timid and nice?

Vita-means.

JACK: A pediatrician is a child doctor.

ZACK: Personally I'd never trust a doctor who wasn't at least twenty-one years old.

MACK: Humph! Don't you know that Pluto isn't a planet anymore?

ZACK: No! And don't bark at me!